513 y

Numbers

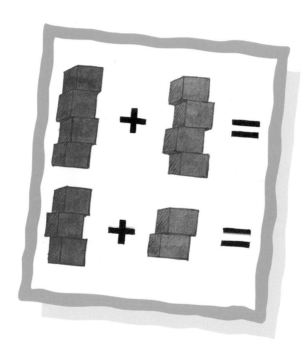

David Kirkby

First published in Great Britain by Heinemann Library
an imprint of Heinemann Publishers (Oxford) Ltd
Halley Court, Jordan Hill, Oxford OX2 8EJ

MADRID ATHENS PARIS
FLORENCE PRAGUE WARSAW
PORTSMOUTH NH CHICAGO SAO PAULO
SINGAPORE TOKYO MELBOURNE AUCKLAND
IBADAN GABERONE JOHANNESBURG

Designed by The Pinpoint Design Company
Printed in China

99 98 97 96 95
10 9 8 7 6 5 4 3 2 1

ISBN 0431 07960 9

British Library Cataloguing in Publication Data available on
request from the British Library.

Acknowledgements
The Publishers would like to thank the following
for the kind loan of equipment and materials
used in this book: Boswells, Oxford; Clarks Shoes; The Sock
Shop; The Early Learning Centre; Lewis', Oxford;
W. H. Smith; N. E. S. Arnold.
Special thanks to the children of St Francis C.E. First School

Photography: Chris Honeywell, Oxford

Cover photograph: Chris Honeywell, Oxford

contents contents

contents

Counting tells you
how many there are.
Here are 5 stars.

Count 3 cars. Count 4 cows.

How many paint pots are there?

How many paintbrushes are there?

To do:
How many paintbrushes
are red?
How many paint pots
are green?

There are different ways of putting numbers in order.

These numbers go round in order.

Are these numbers in order?

To do:
Take a pack of cards.
Remove the picture cards.
Deal out 6 cards.
Put them in order in
a line.
Try again.

You have 10 fingers and thumbs. You also have 10 toes.

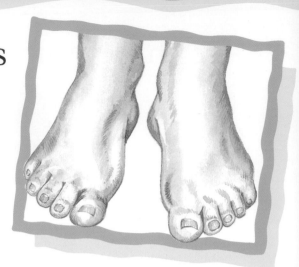

There are 6 fingers and thumbs pointing. There are 4 not pointing.

8

How many balloons
are blown up?

How many
have popped?

How many altogether?

To do:
How many people are
sitting upstairs on the bus?
How many are sitting
downstairs?
How many people are
there altogether?

A pair is a set of 2.

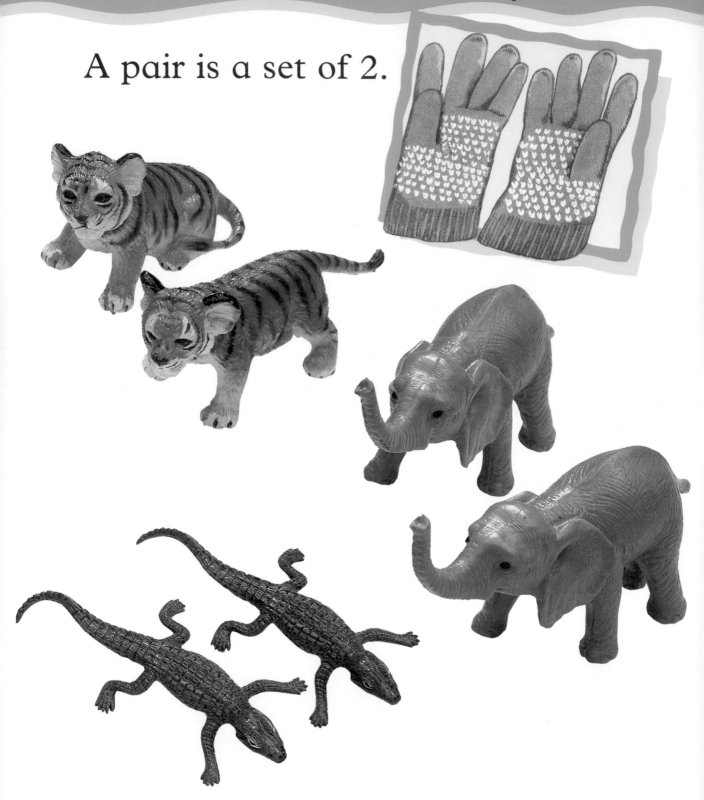

These animals are in pairs.

How many pairs of socks
can you see?

How many pairs of shoes
can you see?

To do:
Look in a mirror.
Can you see any
more pairs?

11

To add 2 and 3 . . .
put them together and count.

$$2 + 3 = 5$$

Count 4 tennis balls
and 2 footballs.
Put them together
and count 6 balls. $4 + 2 = 6$

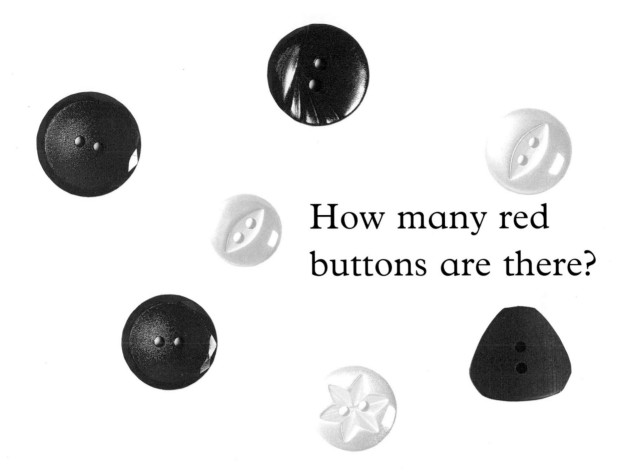

How many red buttons are there?

How many yellow buttons are there?
Add all the buttons together.

To do:
Add together these red and blue bricks.

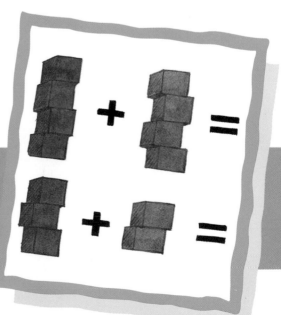

13

These pairs each have a total of 10.

Each pair of cards makes 10.

Which 2 things
can you buy for
exactly 10p?

To do:
Take 6 playing cards.
Find pairs of cards
which make 10.

15

Counting is easier when things are grouped in rows.

Eggs are high in protein, which promotes healthy growth, rich in vitamin B12 for a healthy blood and nervous system, and vitamin D for strong bones and teeth.

The protein is present almost equally in the white and yolk, while the vitamins are more abundant in the yolk. An average egg is composed of 11% shell, 58% white, and 31% yolk.

CARBOHYDRATE	less than 0.1g	less than 0.1g
of which SUGARS	less than 0.1g	less than 0.1g
FAT	10.8g	
of which SATURATES	3.1g	6.9g
MONO-UNSATURATES	4.7n	2.0g
POLYUNSATURATES	1.2g	3.0g
FIBRE	0.0g	0.8g
SODIUM	0.1g	0.0g
		less than 0.1g
AMOUNT OF VITAMINS/MINERALS AND % OF RECOMMENDED DAILY AMOUNT		
VITAMIN D	1.75µg 35%	1.1µg 22%
VITAMIN B12	1.1µg 110%	0.7µg 71%

Do not use damaged or broken eggs. If stored in a refrigerator, remove 30 minutes before use.

These eggs are in 2 rows of 3.

How are these paints grouped?

To do:
Take 12 counters.
Find different ways of
grouping them.

Numbers balance
when the total
is the same
on both sides.

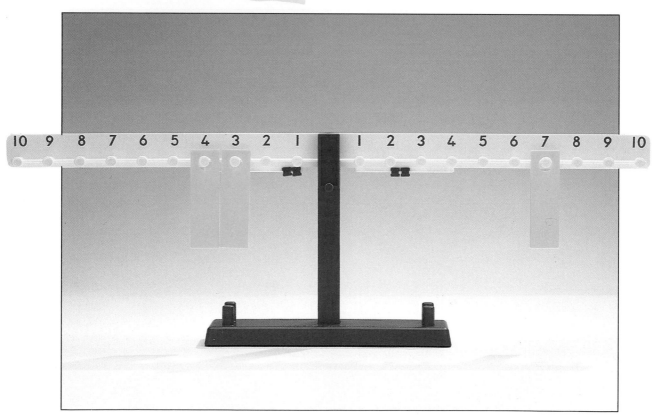

These numbers balance
because   3 + 4 = 7

18

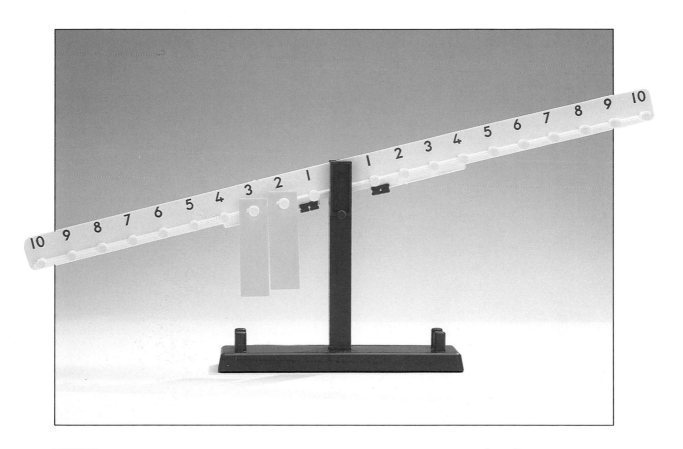

Where can you put one weight to make the numbers balance?

To do:
If one side of a balance has a weight on 6, where can you put 2 weights on the other side?

When you share something equally between 2, you each have a half.

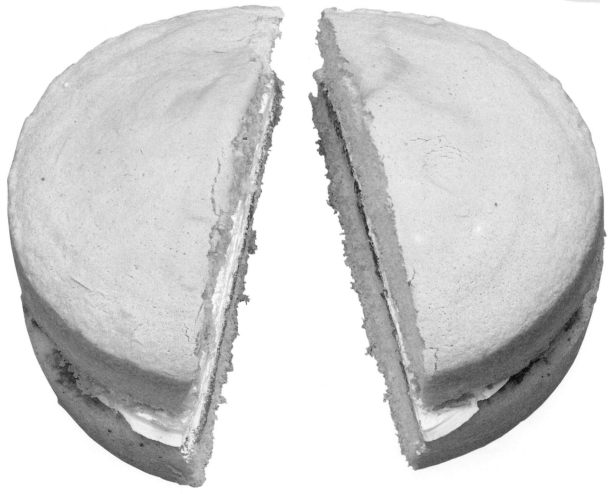

This cake is cut into 2 halves.

How many is half of these plums?

To do:
Fold a piece of paper
into 2 halves.
Can you do this in
different ways?

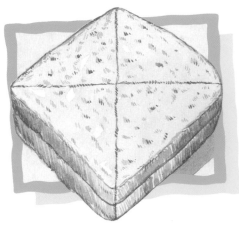

When you share something equally between 4, you each have a quarter.

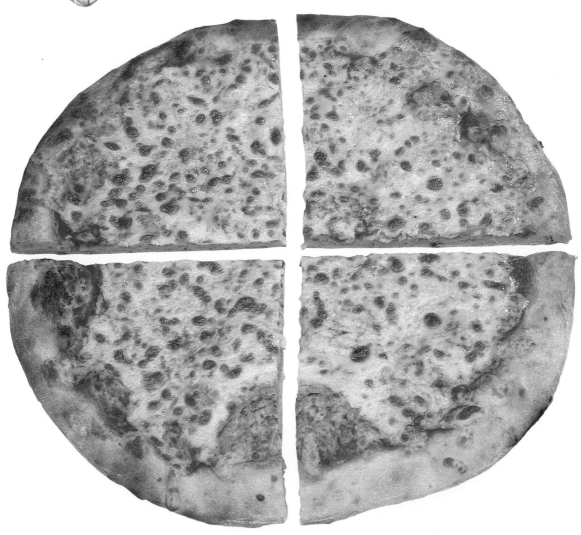

This pizza is cut into 4 quarters.